I0780126

Pink Trees Press

"*The Spellbook of Ordinary Mistakes* is a mesmerizing collection of poems that weaves a tapestry of everyday errors into a spellbinding journey of self-discovery and acceptance. LeCroy transforms mundane missteps into lyrical incantations, exploring the magic inherent in the ordinary and the beauty that arises from imperfection. The journey begins, exploring the questions of destination and purpose, urging readers to navigate their course amidst dragons, fog, and storms. Each poem is a spell, crafted to illuminate the hidden wisdom within and invites readers to embrace the enchantment woven into their fallibility. Through sensual and vivid imagery, she explores the numbing effects of substances and experiences that offer temporary relief while guiding the reader through indulgence, stolen pleasures, and the transient nature of abundance. We are asked to reflect on the dichotomy of curiosity and caution. This inspiring work encourages readers to reflect on their journeys, navigate the storms, savor the honeysuckle of life, and find solace in the shared human experience. It is a celebration of resilience and self-discovery, reminding us that even in our most ordinary mistakes, extraordinary magic is waiting to be discovered."
—**Bernadette McComish,** author of *Florence Nightingale's Lost Log.*

"What I admire in LeCroy's work is that it is void of a certain kind of self-conscious affectation that poisons most everything presented today. It's so in the moment and such an assurance to me that she isn't following or chasing some dream, but that she is the dream itself. In a post-art world, she is a real artist, and that is so rare. She has so much conviction and strength, and it's inspiring." —**Aaron M. Johnson,** poet, jazz musician

"In 'Bouquet,' LeCroy observes: 'What we cease to carry/Carries us through/Write it down.' She writes it down gloriously in this generous exploration of her autobiography, from the first cell that divides to the twenty-four titles in a poem of genius called 'Possible Titles For My Autobiography' inspired by the searing and frank manifestation of what Anais Nin previews in the epigraph 'to find peace with exactly who and what I am.' LeCroy has found that peace. She understands herself. She allows readers the privilege of exploring themselves with LeCroy as their guide." —**Indran Amirthanayagam,** author of *The Migrant States*

"Jane is poetry. Jane is life. Jane is my favorite living poet. When I feel scared of everyone, daunted by rejection, abandoned, gaslit, alienated, and hurting, HUMAN, I find the nurturing poetry of Jane's, and I am reminded that my own spellbook of ordinary mistakes is filled with the everyday magic that keeps a soul from being defeated in the wake of endless struggle that life is. Jane's poetry, exquisitely highlighted in this new collection, is endless solidarity with the choice of life in the face of so much death. I return to Jane's poems the way I do June Jordan or Anais Nin. But Jane is here now, alive!" —**Madigan Shive,** *Bonfire Madigan, radical queer cellist and poet Bonfire Madigan*

"In her first full-length collection in over a decade, Jane LeCroy is as fierce and full of life as ever. The book begins as a striking memoir-in-verse, gathering the details of a cluttered childhood, and turns to a philosophy of our borrowed bodies. LeCroy is a 'pioneer of love,' a poet of

'grand statements,' parsing right from wrong from right, all while reminding us that the blue moon is not really blue. What I love about LeCroy's work is how it encompasses so much: we are simultaneously wounded child and brave warrior woman. 'Trick or Treat,' she writes. 'Trick or Treat./ Both. It's always both.' For LeCroy and her readers, it is always both. Lucky us to have this prophet-poet's reminder."
—**Nicole Callihan,** author of *This Strange Garment*

"This is kind of personal. How not? Over 30 years ago, poet Christian McEwen said, 'You must read this poet' (a student). Jaw dropped. Oh my. That student became my student. She helped my son become an (acclaimed) anti-folk musician dynamo. She's part of our dynamo family dynamic. I've stolen lines from her. She's stolen lines from me (I think). In her poetry, she is constantly stealing my heart. Jane LeCroy is our Jane, a force of nature, a poetic joy. If you haven't seen her perform, no matter. Here, she is on the page, extraordinary and necessary. Should I repeat necessary? Let me do it one more time."
—**Mark Statman**, author of *Hechizo*

Spellbook
of
Ordinary Mistakes

Titles from Pink Trees Press

Silver Tongued Devil Anthology, Linda Kleinbub &
Anthony C. Murphy, Editors
Poems from an Unending Pandemic, Phillip Giambri
Dysfunction: A Play on Words in the Familiar,
Pauline Findlay
Good Boy, Bad Boy, A Better Man, Phillip Giambri
Naming a Hurricane, Madeline Artenberg
The Bookstore Book, Ron Kolm
Spellbook of Ordinary Mistakes, Jane LeCroy

For more information email
Pink Trees Press at PinkTreesPress@gmail.com or
Linda Kleinbub at Linda.Kleinbub@gmail.com

Spellbook
of
Ordinary Mistakes

Jane LeCroy

POEMS

Pink Trees Press

A NOTE ON THE ON THE COVER IMAGE

The original Tappan Zee Bridge was a cantilever bridge spanning the Hudson River, 16,013 feet between Tarrytown and Nyack, where I grew up in the 1970s and 80s. It was opened as part of the New York State thruway on December 15, 1955, and was demolished in a controlled demolition in January 2019. Part was lowered onto a barge and hauled away in May 2019, which I happened to see float by my home in Washington Heights, Manhattan, passing under the George Washington Bridge to be sunk off the coast of the Atlantic Ocean as part of New York State's artificial reef program. The Tappan Zee was designed to last only 50 years due to material shortages during the Korean War at the time of its construction. The Tappan Zee was named for an American Indian tribe from the area called "Tappan," and *zee* is the Dutch word for "sea."

APPRECIATION FROM THE AUTHOR

I thank Pink Trees Press: Linda Kleinbub, Phillip Giambri, Madeline Artenberg, and Pauline Findlay for believing in my work and working with me to make this book exist. I am grateful for the support and encouragement of my family, Dorian, Alice, Laszlo, Luc, my mother, Mary Alice, Jane Girling, and Alethea Hohenberger. I thank all my dear friends who put up with my, "I wrote a poem about it" and let me show them. And I thank YOU for reading my work.
P.S. I love you forever.

Acknowledgments

"A Little Death" *Poetrybay Magazine*
"Add Vice" *The Understanding Between Foxes and Light* (Great Weather for Media)
"Blood Typography" *Suitcase of Chrysanthemums* (Great Weather for Media)
"Dying Wishes" *Silver Tongued Devil Anthology* (Pink Trees Press)
"Exhibition" *Night in the Naked City* (NeuroNautic Press)
"Honeysuckle" *Hanging Loose 101* (Hanging Loose Press)
"I Dreamt You Were Master" *Frank 151 chapter 36*
"Introduction" *Mudfish 7* (Box Turtle Press)
"Molten Core" *Hanging Loose 101* (Hanging Loose Press)
"New York City" *Above the Bridge: First Decade*
"Salmonella Cinderella" *Grabbing the Apple* (JB Stillwater Publishing Company)
"The Ropes" *Hanging Loose 99* (Hanging Loose Press)
"The Tiniest Difference" *From the Inside* (Blue Light Press)
"View-Master" *Hanging Loose 101* (Hanging Loose Press)

"My mission, should I choose to accept it, is to find peace with exactly who and what I am. To take pride in my thoughts, my appearance, my talents, my flaws and to stop this incessant worrying that I can't be loved as I am."
-Anaïs Nin

Contents

We are made of division

From our first cell, we split and keep splitting

Leave what we are, for new leaving,

Dividing, dividing, dividing

Boat

Where is your vessel moored?
I have seen the body
guided by stars
over the natural bodies of water,
how it floats, lists, and bounces as it rests,
how it glides
and unzips the water
as it cuts and goes,
leaving its trail to be swallowed,
its ripples to widen and lap.

What is the map you use?
What is your destination,
or are you one to draw your own
and make the treasure as you go?
Knowing, nothing waits for you
there is only what you drive,
the stars are there for you to use
but they don't care. The planets drift, unfixed
but still trapped in their pattern, repeating.

Your vessel that glimmers in the night
and flashes in the day,
where do you let it take you?
There be dragons
and fog sometimes so thick to steal your vision,
storms and decay besides.
How many sunsets will you get to see?
And between them,
who will you be then
when you anchor,
and then when you are free?

Sad Story

you don't have to suffer
to make great art
but great art is the best
you can make of your suffering,
so, tell your sad story
to the crumpled boxed ears
on the sides of hurt heads
of today and tomorrow
yesterday is a trophy of trials
collecting dust on its shine,
paint and draw your sad pictures
for eyes that float
their corneas in tears,
one tiny boat
out on the black river at night
with a light so little and bright,
I see it from here,
it gets in my poem
and I don't know
to whom that boat belongs
or from where it is or goes,
no matter, the photons
make the poem glow,
the captain sings a song
that makes you cry,
every journey is sad
if you hear it from
beginning to end
listen, picture it
before its light
and after love

The Spoils

the spoils
last for one second
one second
lasts a million years

I want to feed you food
that makes you hungrier
quench you with what
makes you thirst

our beds, we never sleep in
our time, expands as it ticks away

nothing belongs to us
everything is ours
the sky is our ceiling
the world, our map

it is not legal
and it is not wrong
stolen by humans
given by gods

concealed, we are unwrapped
spoken for, we are free

we're spoiled
we're starving
there is no money
the tree is laden with gifts

Introduction

Imagine, I was a child
someone's baby
born, had nightmares
here I am.

Do not introduce yourself
I hate that game,
I don't want to smile
and shake your dick.

I'll invite you home
teach you some tantric sex
if you're flexible.
Impress me.

That boy over there asked me
why I talk so much sex
He wasn't listening
I smile too hard
my teeth are yellow liars.

Cactus

I didn't believe my grandmother's warning
cactus needles weren't a soft aura that
surrounded the cactus in its entirety, like
a veil of still smoke, suspended, I
could not stop myself when
no one was looking I
approached the succulent
on the windowsill with its dust
I reached out to touch
needles that pricked
my skin shocked
in pain my hand
jerked away my
breath taken,
tears sprang
to my eyes,
I swallowed
them, having
been warned
I was 5
years old
and I knew
better-
and I didn't
and I do
to this day
touch
Cact
us

View-Master

Pinocchio, naked
bare blonde wooden boy body
long, capable of elongating
nose

It was a reel
from a set of classic stories
one cell depicted Geppetto beaming
upon his newly erected creation

How it thrilled me to stare
through the keyhole effect
of this most miniature theater
peek at a nude boy

Pulse, applause in my ears
I was caught by this
picture I could not name the curious
way it held me

My red View-Master
thrust into me that first image
to milk from blood, what longing knows-
my heart to pine

Wonderful

My brother found the carcass under the pantry.
We studied the dead, crouched on haunches,
ears like paper flattened to the skull,
wrinkles petrified on the stretched taupe skin, hair gone,
the sunken eyes slit, frozen grimace;
sharp white teeth bared.
The largest carcass we had ever discovered,
mummified, mysterious, unrecognizable, whole;
more exciting than owl pellets or fish
heads hidden in a tree stump by animals.
Spring reveals the earth's dark face, peering
from packed melting snow, life, so dirty, rich.
The crawly things shiny, the carcass matte,
surprisingly weightless as we lifted it
into the large orange Tupperware tub.
Chihuahua? Cat? Raccoon? Skunk?
The most delicate treasure, we carried it carefully
on our laps, on bus 5, to school down King's Highway,
bumps in the road memorized; we didn't let it bounce.
The plastic sarcophagus proudly presented to the teacher,
she didn't know what it was either.
The kids all screwed up their faces and said, "ewwwwww!"
No one seemed to understand.
We had discovered Death and would keep it,
we took it home and loved it for years,
looking under the lid to marvel, often,
the silence of it, the fixed expression.
This discovery was important, we used it
to honor the questions, we let go unanswered.
Even after death, the body is capable of birth,
delivering wonder through the material of time.

More Halloween

I'm from before people were convinced
you had to buy everything.
Halloween, you just pulled together your
witch, hobo, pirate, ghost, monster,
or painstakingly worked on it for weeks,
or Mom did with a sewing machine.
You worried about razors in apples,
poisoned candy, and nuclear war.
Neon was a new color,
you smelled blue fresh dittos damp at school,
most houses had one phone tied to the wall,
you fought over it, TVs were small, no remote,
you learned the Dewey Decimal System,
spent time with typewriters, carbon paper,
microfiche, online is where you waited
at the post office and bank every day,
cassette tape unwound from everywhere
& tangled in trees & blowing in streets
as techno tumbleweeds.
Don't jump, or you'll skip the record.
There's new garbage now,
always plenty to fracking fear.
Will Pop-Rocks mixed with soda
make you explode?
Knock, Knock- Who's there?
Trick or Treat, Trick or Treat
Both. It's always both.

The Ropes

First time I was tied up with rope
was in 3rd grade, he was in 4th
playing *Good Guys vs. Bad Guys*
in the woods after school
who was which never really mattered
just whatever team you were on
we all took the same bus home

Stored props in forts we built we kept
bottles, rocks, spade, ropes, scrap
chasing, laughing, hiding, Andrew
caught me, drew me to him, panting
breathless, red with life suspended
sweat beading diamonds in his dark
velvety crewcut

Our respective teammates scattered,
he focused, I fought, until I had to stop
to catch my breath, he set me up against a tree
clumsily wrapped rope around me
hands behind, shoulders pinned, legs bound
tight and rough it fit a pinching breath
he finished the length of rope, I was tied

He halted to stare at his handiwork,
I stayed quiet, sure to escape
What next? I squirmed, he pushed
his body against mine, inquisitive
racing hearts, our skin touched
breath matched quick
face to face, his tongue licked

my cheeks, my neck,
spontaneous, puppy-like, sweet
perfume of his spit on my skin,
familiar, human, almost comforting,
he stopped, laughed, ran away as if
surprised by his own action, I waited wide-
eyed in the silence of the heat after him

How the licked spots felt cool
tightness on the skin there
every day something new happens
the ropes get shown
a timeline fills with knots
recording, that which releases,
binds

Shed

shed of tiny drawers organizing hardware,
nails, nuts, and bolts, electric powered table saws,
jig saws, workbenches, vices

shed where Opa's whiskey was hidden
beneath floorboards in bleach bottles,
found by Oma who replaced it with piss

shed where accidents happen, slit wrists
along the jagged glass fangs, where little brother's
arm bust through the old single-pane

shed where I feared the exposed fiberglass insulation
like cotton candy stuffing the walls, the room a pink throat,
sweet breath of sawdust, wood residue clinging to sweat

shed where hands numb from constructing, pla80ning,
staining, while Dad cursed the cold, drinking beer,
smoking, complaining the space heater didn't work for shit,
        and warning us kids, to *be careful!*

shed where I made royal crowns from leftover dowels and
scraps from fine chess boards, spice racks, end tables,
wood from cut curves and curly Q's, tacks, glue

shed was a castle, a diner, a pirate ship, a private-eye office
it stored our screens, storm windows, bikes, broken things,
pieces all waiting to be made, fixed, or shed

Dear Piano,

I love how big and beautiful you are. I love your sound;
you are strings, you are percussion. So heavy, you can't be
carried around. You have a crazy shape that gets you
special treatment and, Piano, my favorite thing about you is
that you create the impulse to share; usually wherever you
are- you belong to everyone; you invite everyone to play.
You invite everyone to sit and move their hands all over
your famous black & white keys and step on your brass
pedals. No one can resist touching you as they pass by.
You make us all want to sing. You fill any room you're in.
Out of a room, off stage, you make any landscape look
surreal. I used to curl up under you at my grandma's house
while she played you, and your voice made my whole-body
hum. I am filled with your acoustic electricity, you are
huge, but you can enter me, be through me, transport me. I
used to curl up under your baby grand self when no one
was playing you and feel your hollow weight like a wooden
cloud looming above me on those delicate curvy legs. I was
sure I heard you breathing. Your smooth brass pedals cool
to my hand; when I pushed them, you made a swallowing
sound deep inside you, deep inside me, even though it is
impossible, I know we are in love, even when you're
upright, even spinet at school. You shake my whole-body
and give me goosebumps. Piano, I want to learn how to do
you right. You make me feel so good. Thank you, Piano.

Love, Jane

Honeysuckle

Spring is just winter with a little bit of make-up on
after months of her wet coldness, a blush of color
breaks my heart, teasing me with promises of light.
She finally invites me to take off my coat and pants,
bare my shoulders and legs, wear a short dress, a flag
for the wild ambition that has infused me at the brink
of every summer:
          to collect enough honeysuckle to drink
Determined, I harvest silky luminous little yellow trumpets.
Intoxicated by the scent in a trance from the sweet perfume,
I pluck them one by one from the mess of woody branches,
slay them with my fingertips in a mudra, thumb to pointer
carefully pinching off the bulbous green base, gently
pulling the style through its glistening yellow throat,
dragging the stigma along to flush the honey out.
A single watery drop dripped from each, so tiny
its surface tension fashions a minuscule clear bead
whose immense taste soaks me, flower after
flower thrusting forth from shade each year,
I strive to fill a small cup just a bit, a splash to swish, a sip.
How I hope to be triumphant over an infinitesimal infinity,
the vision of victory through my veins, my blood the same
liquid of life that courses through these days I painstakingly
attempt to collect, dragging pen along paper, pulling ink
down, sweetness so persistent it continually convinces me,
it's possible to savor a swallow, have more than just a taste.
I have yet to succeed; I try and try, a little girl still.

Rain Bonnet

He was the only one who could do her hair;
she got it done once a week, set it
under the bubble hair dryer at Alex's Beauty Parlor.
She used to pass the tic-tacs on her way
to the clear plastic rain bonnet
at the bottom of her purse.
When it was gray and drizzling out,
she would reach in to get it, open it
from its accordion fold, place it
gently over her hair and tie it under her chin
and then give me a white tic tac.
Thank you, Grandma. Now, the rain tastes like mint.

A Generous Impulse

At the toll booth, my mother
paid for the car behind hers.

Once she saw an old man
struggling in the mud, roadside,
and helped him up, and to find his way home.
Later, he took us all to see FANTASIA
at the movie theater
it changed my life, it was so beautiful.

She picked up hitchhikers
and let strangers capture her attention,
honored their sad stories
with empathy and grace.

She befriended the dying,
and welcomed stray souls
to share our food and home.

At the store she let us kids
choose the stick horse
with a broken rein
and a missing eye
because we knew,
no other kids would pick that horse,
and we knew we
would have a good time
with that horse,
that horse needed us kids.
No other kids would do.

Where Are They Now

Those teeth I left under the pillow,
My doll, Rubba Dubba,
I could take in the bath,
Lite-Brite, my View-Master,
the first boy who kissed me -
where are they now?

My first journal, it was gray
with a Jack-in-the-Pulpit on the cover,
my Freezy-Freakies gloves
and Moon Boots from the 1980s,
my beautiful long black coat
that looked like a Victorian dress -
where are they now?

The brown in my hair,
my menses, the babies my children were,
my mother, father, my siblings and their pain,
all the poems and songs -
I will always know where they are.

The macaroni necklace,
my wedding ring -
I hope I don't lose.

Bread and Butter

I only wanted bread and butter.
A natural aversion to every meat
my teeth chewed and chewed,
it never dissolved enough to swallow.

Opa's false teeth flying across the table
to frighten me into eating
on Wednesday nights, family dinner
at my grandparents' with all my aunts and uncles

who were only young adults themselves.
My brother and I were the only children back then.
I grew up in the house my opa grew up in,
his childhood room was my room

where he woke every morning and
walked to the same school I did.
He used a different route, streets changed
when the Tappan Zee Bridge was built.

He loved Port wine and the ocean,
he took us to the beach every year
and told us about the Navy, you got
all new teeth when you joined.

The boys shaved your head the first time
you crossed the equator how
you have no right to complain
you are so lucky and clean your plate.

Everyone snored dozing at the TV, I was not
tired at night and inspected their faces at rest
tried to match their breathing, looked
more closely at the objects in the house-

their mirrored dresser reflecting my face,
Oil of Olay, hairbrushes full of their hair
white doilies covering the surfaces.
My great grandmother had been a lace-maker

from the old country and is said to have made
table linens for the Whitehouse and if they
are not there, where would they be?
I watched the Tappan Zee bridge get replaced.

Opa's teeth, my teeth, changing places
all the things outplaced, the bridges
like steel lace flying across the table
chew and chew but cannot swallow.

Father's Day

My father was a drug dealer on our dead-end street,
Eminent Domain for the New York State Thruway.
He was always drinking Pabst Blue Ribbon
day and night but I only saw him really drunk
a few times.

He drove an old police car, rust-patched
with swaths of rust-colored primer.
It was one of my chores to clean the blue interior,
soft cloth the ripped dashboard, and torn vinyl bench seats.
He insisted that tattered car be clean.

Once in early June, air thick with honeysuckle,
I made a mistake, shooting the ArmorAll
straight into my eye. I ran from the car screaming in pain
across the lawn ravaged by the neighbor's chickens
but still planted with grass seed in hope every spring.

My father was wielding the garden hose,
cleaning the screens to dress the windows for summer,
scrub brushing away the orangish stained glass mosaics
of fly shit left from last year, pixelating the mesh.

He tilted my head back and flushed out my eye
with the powerful force of water.
My eye ached and stung, he managed to rinse it,
I didn't go blind.
My head fit into his hand.

In the Desert

My childhood landscape being torn down before my eyes,
goodbye goodbye. Glass towers rise, erase the broad sky.
My grandparents watched the Tappan Zee bridge go up;
now, they're gone as I watch that same bridge come down,
replaced because the original was beyond repair.
We must dedicate ourselves to improvement or perish.
The fact I prefer burnt, room-temperature leftovers eaten
over the sink, to fine dining, is evidence I was raised by a
drug addict. That house that protected me from the snow
and rain is the same house that hurt me with generations of
pain, eminent domain. Reached middle age working to get
all my ducks in a row, but it turns out this carnival is a
shooting gallery and I lose. Life is ugly. Everything is hard
and there's no winning. Deserve the punishment this life is,
fit the crime like a glove.

That's blunt and much too negative, darling, I apologize.
It grates on the nerves like rich kids throwing around the
word *boring*. If you can identify the problem, you're
halfway to the solution. Hmmm. You think it's a heart of
gold I have? No. It's only gold veneer, inside it's just a
muscle, a bloody thing, alive. I like it, I really do. Eat it.
Like in the famous poem. You know the one.

Do All Roads Lead Home?

The Henry Hudson Parkway
outside my apartment
is getting redone.
The toxic black smell of tar
wafts up through my windows,
I breathe it in deep, loving it,
I fill myself; I can't get enough.
I mention my affinity to my husband.
Below, steamrollers powerfully crush along,
electrical hum buzzing through me.
I feel it in my heart.
He says it's because I grew up
on the New York State Thruway.
I relay the story to my brother,
who reminds me our neighbor was a roofer
whose workshop exhaled that same exhaust.
Scents swirl, slip, slick, make sense.
The poisons we grow up with
become the poultices of the soul.

Life During Wartime

My grandmother couldn't afford stockings,
marked a line up the back of her legs instead,
so it looked like she had them on.
It was a mistake to dance with the black soldiers
in port for the week at the big USO event,
they were badly beaten afterward.
How many acts of kind appreciation result in horror?

My grandfather only wore long pants, a bayonet scar
marked the length of the back of his leg.
I caught glimpses of it a couple times. Whoever
gave it to him was upholding something beloved, too.
He had stories: pugilist, tap-dancer, motor pool, gardener,
but only told what he wanted to tell.

He rarely answered my questions or elaborated
on what interested me most: the scar, and
how he slept warm enough in the icehouse
he protected at night for the family business, and
were there pushcart wars and electric cars
and farms uptown in New York City?
Maybe humans shouldn't be saved;
we should perish. Earth, better off without us.

A little drunk, but I remember paying the bartender,
my head swarming with war stories. Who is the bad guy,
according to whom? Stumbling onto the same streets
as my grandparents 100 years ago. Life during wartime
is always, always a war, always fighting, and more alcohol.
There's no such thing as better off.

The World Ends Every Day

air strikes match chemo psycho therapy
can't sleep, just dream boat sinks loose
leaf falls off tree top spins the bottle breaks the heart
brakes fail safe as houses crack your head aches
and leaks oil blood money gas water time out you go
in with the new digs a grave stone's throw up your arms
race car crash test dummy up fool's gold standard run of
the mill house of cards play the hand you're dealt
it's the best you can do your best no one gets to be happy
only for moments
the world ends every day

Childhood Games

Playing flashlight-tag with the boys
in the old, abandoned paper mill on the river
They were stronger and faster but I could still catch them

When it was my turn, I'd hide to seek, I'd wait for the boys
to get restless with hiding, so they'd venture out
and I grabbed them with my beam

shining among the crumbling edges, to break
the empty shadows into walls with skin of peeling paint
and swirling halos of dust particulate in the air

Floodlights meant to deter trespassers deterred us not at all,
lured by the darkness to outline us into drawings of light
as if we were angels, like we'd never get hurt

I didn't even drink whiskey back then
and I was so drunk I almost died
dropped through a hole on the roof

Some shaft, or a staircase whose stairs were gone
that went all the way down five oversized stories
to the basement, the smell of damp cement and mold

My friend caught my wrist, I dangled cartoon-like,
he lifted me up, my life was saved, our hearts pounding,
we laughed, we laughed at our victory

All our wars reduced to games in the night
of varying risks and costs, and we hope
someone catches us

Solicitation

I discovered the meaning
of the word "virginity"
and I was on a mission
to get rid of that
inexperience
did not appeal to me, 13,
at a Christian sleep-away camp
in New Hampshire. I wrote a letter
to Jacob Cane at home in New York,
explaining we didn't have to be in love,
we could just practice on each other.
I used pencil and loose-leaf,
Pachelbel's Canon in D, fingers on keys
described the bath I could give to him,
a fort in the woods we could hide away,
experiment and play, offer critique
so we'd be good at it
when we needed it to count.
His father discovered El Nino,
my father worked in a warehouse.
Lanky poet outcast woos pudgy valedictorian.
I licked the stamp, sent the letter
but he never took me up on my offer.
We never kissed, or squeezed, or tried,
never held hands; sent him sand.
Now, grown with children of our own,
we both wear rings.
It's still in a box under his bed,
precious things.

The Old Fashioned

So, they wouldn't kill my father,
so, he wouldn't kill himself,
I worked at the Mafia-run restaurant
almost every day after school
my father would come in to drink
and give me a kiss as if he loved me
as if I were getting paid to work there
as if daughters were for cocaine debts
as if I didn't have homework to do

His friends would slip twenties in my pockets,
fifties came from Billy and those sorry men
flashing their sad smiles, I always smiled back
and said everything was fine as I watched them
take the same seats every night
to root for the same team as they drank the same
cursing, laughing, smoking, snorting

The greasy kitchen and cigarette smoke
saturated my uniform, the smell never left
I threw those clothes away
I'm glad I'm not a kid anymore

Window Dressing

When I worked as a teen
at The Old Fashioned restaurant
Joe, the owner, gave instructions

in his New York, wise-guy voice:
Ya see the front tables
inna windows there?— sweeping

his arms from the mountain of his body,
gesture at the prime spots
visible from the sidewalk on Broadway—

Don't let any fat fucks sit there.
They come in,
you seat 'em inna back.

A cigarette toggled
on his lower lip
as if glued in place. I nodded,

compliant. *Tables one, six, and twelve,*
I don't wan' fat fucks
ova there. Put nice, good lookin'

people inna windows. An' keep
the ashtrays empty. I d'wanna
see no butts on the tables.

I understood.

Joe was a fat fuck.

Heart Transplant

I hated when he carried his gun
in his sweatpants pocket, it was so obvious;
like he was asking to go to jail-
walking around slovenly armed.

A man like that doesn't get to live long
and when he had his heart attack at 47
I was not surprised.
Would he wear sweatpants in his coffin?

His mother would decide
from behind her mask of tears
but he didn't die, he lived to have a heart transplant.
After that, he was a changed man:

he didn't have the same favorite color
he didn't laugh at the jokes he used to like
he never played with his gun
he didn't even kiss the way he used to

Death comes with the scythe and a bag of money
but sometimes Death comes with the scythe and
a second chance.
No matter, the scythe is always there.

Add Vice

What are you using
to rip out your eyes-
so you don't have to look?

What drug, what drink
makes it all go away-
what lips, whose kiss?

What kind of touch
makes it bearable-
the feather, the whip?

The horror of the everyday,
the repetition, the stark replay.
What song do you listen to?

With whom do you dance?
Lips numb from whiskey,
eyes smoke

In Their Early 50s

Peter Green was the first of my dad's friends to die.
It wasn't just the copious amounts of cocaine
that the 80s blew up their noses, it was
the combination of that with other things:
alcohol, tobacco, cholesterol, humanity, denial
makes it hard to breathe, he was 50 when he stopped.
Pneumonia, sitting upright in a rocking chair, refusing
to go to a doctor because he knew there was no cure
for ghosts, impulses of youth that haunt the body, hiding
days away so you never get old, just sick soon, fade fast.
He chose home over a hospital,
                              always one to self-medicate,
It's a free country but lots of drugs are illegal
and the black market with black eyes and black lungs-
Can you blame someone for trying to find their own way?

God's Eyes

It was a golden time, nothing could hurt us, sugar
and tobacco were safe, STDs wouldn't kill you,
God's Eyes were watching in the 1970s,
colorful yarn diamond spun around two crossed sticks
hung in every home, as did macramé and wallpaper.
Everyone did street drugs back then, prescriptions
hadn't won the self-help pleasure market. Kids
don't make ashtrays at school for their parents anymore.
There was a phone number you could call to get the time.
Coming of age in the 1980s, AIDS was the buzzkill
of the Sexual Revolution, sex death epidemic.
When I was a teenager, everyone used to think
I was my father's girlfriend when we were out;
strangers dropped their jaws when I addressed him,
Dad. His long hair under his halo of a headband doo-rag,
paraphernalia all around the house, mirrored tables,
rolled up dollar bills, pornography taped to walls and
stacked in piles, VHS, and a wall of vinyl records.
Synthesizers delivered the new music.
Remarkable women he loved, including my mother, left
their things behind, relics. But when you move out of a
house, never to return, the house stays in you,
an intangible landscape of knots, paper, leftover Gods
eyes.

Junior High

They told me my features were my flaws.
They said I was wrong and they said I was ugly.
I said, "Now, I will never ever kiss you."

He stood there dumb, the class squirmed
as I stood fast and offered a rejection
to an invitation I never received.

The school years passed like that-
they shunned my shoes,
by senior year they all had a pair.

Signing my yearbook with apologies and praise
to shine their own faces. Politics, social strata
laid bare in these initial petty tribulations.

I left them all behind
and kept them with me;
that, my skin.

Accordion

for GFH

No matter what, the accordion has
such a sad sound
the weight of it against your chest
heartbreaking, pump the life into it
the straps around both your shoulders
its peculiar breathing, a party
buttons and keys galore
its case a valise

Music holds you, the instrument
teaches you how to hold it, impedimenta

The guitar chameleon's emotions
amplify any mood with that long neck
the hollow body, rigid
sits upon your lap or hangs
from just one shoulder
its vibrating strings sing a chorus
"Pick me"
its case a coffin

He saved up for it himself, as a kid
his brothers played accordion
but my father insisted on guitar
he learned it well but he swore
they hated him for it
for following his own
impulse and desire
for making his case

Radial Symmetry

I have seen the face of Death
with its cancer eyes, car crash-nose,
ears of self-destruction: drugs and suicide,
heart-attack teeth, auto-immune-disease mouth,
lines of organ failure and the tongue of starvation,
the hair of eternal sleep
Oh, accident!

Heart of disappointment
disappointed heart
beating its beats beaten downtrodden
lift, lift up like a ski lift lifts
legs dangling in the cold over the white
lift, lift up like a hot air balloon
life guided in a wicker basket by a giant roaring flame
lift, lift up like an alien abduction in a beam of light

Little hands, please
remove the face of Death
take off the head, be out of your mind-
just be the body
like some starfish missing an arm
that was recently removed and is already regenerating
and the lone broken piece becoming another starfish too,
clinging to the rocks in the rough sea

Dying Wishes

He's holding a beer, in most every memory I have of him,
my childhood cluttered with the bottles,
                                    multiplying, metastasizing
after decades of alcohol and cocaine, he was 14 years clean
but only morphine could relieve the pain—
                        stage four at 54—pancreatic cancer.
He needed too much dope to die at home;
so, he was admitted into a hospice where kindly, retired
firemen strolled the halls, pushing a cart of top-shelf liquor
and everything besides, to comfort the dying
and those who love them: vodka, fine whiskey, wine, gin
and even Pabst Blue Ribbon, his old staple, the piss
draining from his body through a tube, color of Guinness.
Now, during his last nights on Earth,
                        I encouraged him to have a drink,
he had enjoyed it so much once upon a time.
"No," he said, as the IV drip trickled above his bed,
machine blinking MORPHINE over his head,
"I'm dying sober."

Perennials

The flowers in the vase with water
that he gave to you to make you smile,
drop a mess of detritus mimicking the rot of teeth,
sweet scent soon stench of decay,
flowers will be thrown away

It was practically a burden to receive flowers,
peonies wilting quickly to a limp ombre'
spilling ants on my table,
more chore than gift
I'd dread

the present of flowers,
blooms emblem of loss:
flowers when you're sick,
flowers when you're sorry
as a gesture of love, they forewarn decline
(ask the bride and groom 10 years later)
a traditional comfort at funerals

From his yard, my father brought me
forsythia for my birthday,
lilacs for Mother's Day,
I threw those flowers away
as many times as I got them

Now that he is dead,
those flowers deliver him
from buds, from branches, from roots,
recursive memory's bouquet
and nothing to throw away

Estate Sale

Invisible wind, give us directions,
some people came for a weathervane
and they left with all the everyday silverware

Others came and bought the sheets for a dollar,
filled them with my mother's wedding china and crystal,
sneaking out the bundles, I pretended not to see

The estate sale that went on for a year,
doling out the trash, the treasure
(it's all the same, one man's life)

We were wrong about how many dumpsters we'd fill,
how long it would take, what was worth the most:
vinyl records, porn magazines, guitars

Death, *memento mori*
my mother cried and cried
as if it were a personal affront, robbery

I explained I don't have room for china and crystal,
and neither do my brothers or you, Mom
we left this at Dad's for 19 years

so, this is all just garbage anyway,
we need more room in the dumpster,
there's always more shit to throw away

Soothsayer

I sat at the psychic's table,
she had a ring on every finger that clicked a Morse code
as she sifted through the cards piecing together the story.

The stars at my birth gave us their math,
she expanded it into my history and future,
the love and deception that made me.

It was a narwhal's tusk, not a unicorn's horn.
How can she know, when we can't even predict weather,
or be sure of our origin?

The man I thought was my father, was not.
We don't get to choose the lines on our palms,
and the crystal ball only reflects the room it's in,
                                    upside down.

She tells everyone the same thing:
something they want to hear
                        and something they are afraid of,
"He's still your father, and there's another."

Molten Core

I've never been Earth's molten core
but I have been angry enough to burn with a heat
that liquefies the edges of my center, to bubble up through
the surface, erupting into full-fledged fights
that break hearts, changing the face of my world

I've never been Earth's molten core
but my insides are also only conceptualized,
the physical self is all educated guesses and artist renditions
measured by high-tech tools and metaphors,
never openly exposed enough for actual air to rush through

I've never been Earth's molten core
but my passion has blazed to reveal seismic mysteries
beyond the primordial soup, conjuring an origin
outside of Time as we know it, existing supernaturally
though grounded as the ground itself

I've never been Earth's molten core
but I have pushed whole people from my body
created by my own iron-rich blood, a part of
ancient recipes and no one can name all the ingredients
that came from the stars

Lunatics

It came from dreams, it should have been kinder but
we all know what happened after we got to Easter Island.
Only the insane would attempt the voyages
that made our world.

Polynesians found Hawaii using double-hulled canoes,
set out blindly on the open ocean. Surely, many more died
trying than those that reached the shore.
What is the price of paradise?

Mad Magellan with a messiah complex
circumnavigating the Earth shaped like a breast
according to crazy Columbus,
delusional slave trader, guilty of genocide.

My own father abused me, my country riddled with laws
showing disdain for me and what I hold dear.
Hudson was so obsessed with the Northwest Passage
his crew mutinied, stranding him near the arctic.

Our hearts cold, our minds on fire.
Who would spend billions of dollars
to go to the moon, when people are starving
on Earth, dying of diseases that money can cure?

I admit it, I would. I would.
I do not forgive the explorers the horrors of their crimes
but I know I am one of them, guilty
of my wildest dreams.

I Want

to walk in the snow with you
the fat snowflakes slapping our faces
I want to feel the world with you
hand in hand and have you
in my arms sleep next to you I want to tell you
all the things I think about and listen hear
you here I want to watch the scene the sea the graffiti
birds and flowers the way branches twist and point
the lace of the waves I want to draw
you naked the way you hunch over a little
your muscular body you always have
something to do you have plans always
at the helm, you navigate through
every kind of water I do my best
to hold on

Blood Typography

Everyone wishes the Golden Gate Bridge were golden
and the constellations were more convincing pictures,
but some insist they can read your stars and your palm.
Didn't you know, you can confess to a Jack-in-the-pulpit
if you're a good enough poet to fill in the blanks
with bullet points and yawns so big they break your jaw
like candy no grown-up dares to eat because
you only look forward to losing that first set of teeth.
Your DNA is not the only artist rendering you.
Blueprints were blue, back when we had contact
with contact print. Before we started sending objects
and lights to the stars, we just received their light
and put our gods there with names, each a story.
Be the mighty farmer of your window box,
plow and weed and plant some kind of small expanse,
whatever you can manage with the whiskey
on your lips and the wine running down your legs
like the blood of Christ at mass and eat of my body
says every mother that does the natural thing
and spills the golden gate the milky way
into the tiny face of the biggest heartbreak
that little love letter about the birds and the bees.
Finally, a little flower you get to name.
Just remember, the blue moon is not really blue.

Manhattan Bridge

We both got around the city
him, on his fancy custom track bike
me, on my cheap factory girl's bike
him, rich; ashamed of his privilege and wealth
me, poor; wearing my common struggle like a badge
both costumes so typical, tawdry
our vehicles chained to the walkway fence
of the Manhattan Bridge our hearts chained too
my heart is not factory-made or cheap
his heart had brakes and breaks
the metaphor only goes so far
but we went so far to where no one was imagining
stole up the suspension cables in the dark of night
we climbed up inside the bridge
the precarious ladder stapled
up along the innards of the towers
lovers always feel so original
though that ladder *was* built there,
proof it has all been imagined before
336 feet in the air we emerged over our city
in a heap of fist-sized bolts and safety-yellow power tools
bridge maintenance means constant repair
soaring above the city's main river artery
perched above all the refuse and light
we told one another we thought the other so beautiful
we kissed a kiss so hard we became one love being
that exists still, despite the fact we do not,
we climbed back down, unlocked our bikes
for hot chocolate in Chinatown
went back to Brooklyn to sleep together a knotted nest
our glory of togetherness lasted about 336 days
this is what we have left

Gobstopper

The room looks new
but one chipped piece of paint
reveals the layers of color
that the wall had been over time
like a rainbow gobstopper
most of the pain was older than me
even my own pain
older than me
because
my first two relationships
were mine with my mother
and my father
they were new parents
but one tiny flaw revealed layers
of color
pain layered on them
from before their own births
and in my mouth my cells reveal
my DNA that holds the blue
print for the gobstopper
rainbow reign that I try
to dissolve in my mouth
I can't break through with my teeth
this life is a jawbreaker
and we are trapped in this room
that seems to be new
but it's not
it is old, older than
our cells
making it hard to forgive
ourselves

Possible Titles for My Autobiography

Mysterious Punishments
The Life and Times I Fucked Up
Impossible Solutions
The Way to Live on Salsa, Chips, Cheese, and Apples
Not Who You Think You Are
Consequences of Tragic Superpowers
How to Break Your Face
Looking Under Rocks
Repeat Defeat
The Disease that is Being Human
I Came to Fail
Unmarketable
Spellbook of Ordinary Mistakes
Feral Child Through the Years
Can't Help It
Hating is Caring
No Great Expectations
Not Feeling Better Yet
Side Effects of the Grand Equivocator
Pendulum of the Pain Plane
I Can't Believe I Didn't Die
Loving Outside the Lines
How to Rent Rooms by the Hour
No Regrets, Not Sorry

Love

Love hurts it smarts it makes you stupid
it pains pricks pounds pierces punches
makes you sick horny happy hungry full
it hurts the worst it hurts the best
you felt it you feel it you came from it
you go to it you can't live without it
over and over it keeps coming
it asks of you it tells you you fear it
you know it you want it you want more
you are a slave to it it controls you
if you say it doesn't you're lying
you do anything for it be foolish be brave
you get it you lose it you fall in and out
your heart is your motor the organ of Love
because heart makes us live it's what we use
to measure life it's our ruler and ruler and rule
it takes our breath away it makes us breathe fast
it makes us breaks us shakes us wakes us
and if you try to avoid it you get ugly and mean
give in given give love you know what I mean

I Dreamt You Were Master

I dreamt you were master
bating the moon
the Milky Way shot from you.

To swallow these stars
is to glow with your light,
this infinite joy
be   coming   night.

I look at clear skies
during dark, spilling stars
in slow motion
I am   yours.

Though light
years we may be
a part
our love is art.
The sky is stained
with our hearts.

Like the face of Christ
on The Shroud of Turin
the stories are gorgeous
beyond religion.
Greeks believed Night's face
was milk from a breast,
I put white drops
upon your lips I kissed
and kiss still
your image impressed my eye,
telescope fulfilled.

Myogenesis

You must cut the heart out of such things
I have been advised
to not prescribe so much meaning
to the illicit pleasure of our bodies together

Knives can't cut words though
the tongue does, the muscular hydrostat
like the octopus tentacle
or the elephant trunk

The heart is a muscle too
but words are stronger, live longer
Are words themselves abstract nouns?
Without words, the heart is only a muscle

Our bodies of muscle and bone
hold thoughts, perform actions,
love,
I will not cut the words out

In the beginning, was the Word,
without words,
what belongs to us,
how do we give or prove it?

What's a tentacle, trunk, tongue for?
Metaphor me
that which we cannot touch
that which we cannot cut

the heart
out of such things

Carving Station

The surgeon understands what the butcher does
the butcher understands the surgeon
white coat, white apron, red blood
Cut open

Take a number
wait on line, drain fluid, slice
of life, everybody knows the knife
One saves, one slaughters, both fill their orders

Laid out
paper to catch the mess
beast on beast, breast to breast
Familiar instruments in each chest

A test
to pass for any collar, apprentice, or scholar
one paid by the pound, one by the hour
Sometimes I am one, sometimes the other

What I Learned from Him

Sophisticate fruition of your yearning,
play a patient game, life is as slow as it is quick
we have more time than we think, less than we know,
a couple hours last forever, years tick by in a wink,
the flow, clocks lie, we can cheat
we can sneak in more to have, more to remember
in stairwells and doorways, storage lockers underground,
on riverbanks, bathrooms in bars,
boss' beds, empty apartments, cars
Glory! But what good is
sex without love? I'll tell you,
you cannot cut the heart out of such things,
it's the heart that makes the things the things,
let the ages crawl along, squeeze out
a girlfriend, a spouse, a child, a lover
we are instruments of detection of the self
through the other, steady input, trial and error,
days lovely mistakes we dream away,
wander the streets, wonder if this is awake or asleep,
the pendulum relentless, it's our burden
to make sense of it all, keep some mystery of the self
for the self, so we have more to give away later, show
You get a few years, then poof

That I can never recall your exact face when we are apart,
or the sequence of events in which we lay our swollen
pink bodies of time side by side for the exchange—
secret friend, my brother, my equal—but nonetheless
drawn asunder, perpetually at the point of collapse,
only proves how we are meant to remain, withstand,
crawl through days with heart,
just as I push all the levers at once, staining your shirt

Two Tone

Maybe it's our bilateral symmetry,
mirror-like, that makes us seek pairs.

Reflection is a backwards repetition,
duplicates, doubles echoing.

We like them, look for them,
seek a match, attach.

Dice, knitting needles, oars, together they're more.
Eyes, hands, feet, kidneys, lungs, in pairs they come.

One coin, two sides, right-side-up/upside-down
in/out, dark/light, hot/cold, left/right.

Opposites and twins are pairs,
a general invariance, two facets of the same force.

A bond displays strength separated,
        gravity and acceleration;
a physical law expressed
        in a generally covariant fashion,
        takes the same mathematical form
        in all coordinate systems.

Electricity and magnetism, two complementary aspects
of electromagnetism, a more fundamental force.

Starboard.
Port.

Salmonella Cinderella

Salmonella Cinderella
She's the beast, he's the belle
He's the beau, she's the show
She says yes, he says no

Thinking king of hearts he is,
She's the card right under his

I read your mind, never mind
Always your deck, never mine
Hours ours, for hours and hours
We go together like funeral & flowers

To Dye Your Heart

Love is free, but can you afford it?
Mysterious as an egg
to conceal to be concealed,
heart nestled in its cage,
in its nest of organs,
a mansion with only four chambers,
another fist-sized universe,
delicate, motor, metaphor.
We draw it as clean lines,
traditional valentines,
to avoid the real bloody thing,
disciplined to disguise it, seduced
by limitations and their deception of ease.
We are convinced to regulate
the flow of love, as if love were finite
we dye the heart to participate
in irresistible social games.
We hide it, obsessed with pairs,
one heart to seek one other.
My heart too big to hide, no match
you know, you have seen it, tasted it,
my heart has grown, been broken
open, and a fantastic menagerie
parades forth, creatures that want
to roam and lick and chase, are punished
like monsters, forced into cages,
shut up like eggs to be hidden
The possibility to be wild and huge
is rejected in this visceral dream
that is culture,
I long for a new Easter.

Study in Blue Economics

Your worth is untranslatable to a wage.
Your inherent value is greater than
any measurement device could interpret.

Earnings, simply a myopic mercantilism,
pressure to quantify, justify, goals, plans.
You cannot understand how heavy a heart is
by weighing it, or know how big it is by noting metrics.

Poetry is the most accurate tool we have
to calculate the size and weight of this life, melting
Dali clocks imparting the erratic lengths of our hours
like dreams.

Think of sunlight spooling through your shirt,
undressing you beneath your clothes
to survey the edges defining your form
to wear its warm and weightless veil.

I complied to be taken in a picture,
gladly, to pause, pose, be captured,
to keep this communion in light
the way time travels.

We didn't come to Earth to pay bills,
trade in our heartbeats for cash.
There's no saving up days in the bank,
better safe on a river,

like that night we spent on the riprap Hudson shore,
opposite glittering Manhattan, where clothes were removed
and we wore the great skyline, still too small to cover us.

Prize

It's not true that whoever dies with the most money, wins
Bend at your knees so they can't look up your dress
Draw on fake eyebrows, feel gorgeous, they'll believe you
Repetition convinces everyone, religion proves it
Sneeze in the crook of your arm so you don't spread germs
All our grievances are connected
If you let your wild eyebrows connect and feel sexy, it is
Everyone knows a smoker who lived to 93 and
        a non-smoker who died young of cancer
You can't figure it out and nothing is fair
If you choose the Kaiser roll that's been sitting next to
        the donuts, it tastes like a donut
Paint doesn't fix things, it just makes them look better
Whitewash the hours with near misses and you hit the mark
Pain doesn't enhance things, it just makes them meaningful
The target is bigger than it looks,
        you're better than you think
The end is stuck to the beginning,
        it never helps to isolate them
All our loss is a consequence of our abundance
Whoever dies with the most tricks
        up their ripped-apart sleeves, that's who wins
The prize is the game
No need to compete

King of the Sea

He has been roughing me up every day,
braiding and unbraiding my hair, making me wet.
We do this every summer.

He pulls me into him, pushes me around in his huge arms,
his salt washes all over me in a way that puckers my skin
from his encompassing kisses, we're tight like that.

He catches me the way branches hold the moon, wraps me
in cool white lace, tumbles me onto the beach, leaves me
exhausted from our wrestling, his liquid trickling out of me.

Remember when he propped me on your finger
and made me forget the world and time? A mermaid,
I floated there, buoyant, rising out of your hand.

He spun me onto your sex, a transgression.
You had to shake me back into my human form,
this life of limits & consequence.

You asked if I was dreaming or teasing.

Dreaming, I was dreaming awake with you, Neptune
stuck our hearts with his trident, just to get
a little of our blood mixed
into the sea.

How to be a Pioneer of Love

Expand the heart, love more
Practice love in secret, publicly proclaim love
Love as much as you can
Do whatever it takes to experience love
Say yes to love every time it offers itself to you
Take Cupid's poisonous arrows
Incorporate that poison into everything you do
Reject belief in a limited capacity of the human heart
Never try to own another
Never let yourself be owned
Worship and adore as many as you can
Open your body and mind to lovers
Suffer the consequences
Give yourself away
Cry, laugh, orgasm, act on your dreams
Reject the impossibility, revel in the rebellion
Tear apart the fabric of society
Recognize your broken heart, accept pulverization
Accept failure and loss and triumph
Break more, fail more, lose more, triumph more
Live & love until there's nothing left of you
Write all the love letters you can
Seduce seduce seduce & be seduced
Conduct the electricity that is the life pulse
Don't deny yourself Earthly pleasures
Give yourself permission to love to death because
We're all going to die, and before we die, we can love
Fall in love often, stumble, trip, CRUSH
Even though it beats you the hardest, wrecks you
      and leaves you in shambles,
All we have are shambles
Everything is an illusion, so what?

Then illusions are enough
Love mortifies you, it enslaves and sets you free
You will rise again
Practice rejecting possessiveness
Banish jealousy, try and try
Loving adds more meaning to every action every day
It makes every hour worth more than 60 minutes
Fit more living into your life
            by playing on the frontier of love
Be shot down and destroyed
Be exalted and praised
You cannot protect yourself, even if you live hiding
You will suffer the consequences of love
So just stand up and love
There is a math & physics beyond this defined realm
There are no maps but what your lover's hair
            draws upon your skin
It is always changing,
            like the surface of the unknowable ocean
Let this terrify you, be terrifying
Join this army
Set examples
On fire

X

We would kiss until our faces were raw, until it hurt, stung,
numbed, our faces red from kissing, our lips tenderized as
succulent meat hammered by the grid of metal points on a
kitchen hammer, our hearts beating so fast it felt like we
were birds, the whole world dissolved into the kissing, our
teeth were castles in our mouths dissolving like candy, our
tongues Valentines and Chinese New Year and 4th of July,
our palates diving boards in scary dreams, off cliffs into
rivers concealed with fog, our throats passages to other
dimensions, our tonsils curtains opening upon grand theater
stages, the insides of our cheeks were slip-n'-slides in yards
of childhood, it was psychedelic, hallucinogenic,
it defied time, it was supernatural, extraterrestrial, it is still
happening, those kisses, they are eternal, we were drinking
each other, eating each other, loving each other,
worshipping each other, igniting each other, extinguishing
each other, it was so wet, delicious, sexy, fun, irreverent,
holy, it is famous in my life, it is a lighthouse that warns all
the other ships that there are edges, there are rocks, it is
dangerous, but you have no choice when you find yourself
in that wild water, steer with your heart, be guided by the
light erected in honor, you can never drop anchor and stay
in one place but there is the map and the memory, the
blood, the wounds, the scars, the story of that eternal kiss
shaping your face, the way the weather shapes the cliffs of
the sea, so harsh, so beautiful, so grand we are humbled, we
are awed, we are staring into the face of change, formed,
transformed, born and buried by love

Pink

Toxin from their diet of shrimp,
once processed, makes flamingo plumage
famously pink

Whiskey compromises vision
but paints the world a fine and pleasing
impressionism

Their painted teeth and nails did glow
Radium Girls; Marie Curie's prize
reminds me of you

What makes life so lovely,
poisons us too

New York City

Sometimes undone the icing has me
She is a lovely New York City
with river limbs dangling sparkling bangles of bridges,
the ocean grabs her feet, her edges are beaches
      I wish I didn't want her
Her luminous starless nights,
glowing skyline oscilloscope reading of life,
Her staring holy moon, her extremes of temperature:
burning, freezing, lovely, I want to be her thermometer-
She leaves me begging always wanting always having
always imagining more, I am in awe of her I need a rest
from her, I long for her, long New York City
      I wish I didn't want her
A bicycle licks her in less than a day
but the life of an eye cannot know her entirety, entirely
her incessant construction, destruction, traffic pulse,
ribbons of lanes, veins of underground trains
teeming with dreams, garbage, and smells,
covered with sores, wounds, riches, and bells,
wildlife, wild life, we claim to know her well,
giant concrete wishing well
      I wish I didn't want her
eight million strange strangers each have their own vision
beyond truth, beyond fiction, temptation, religion,
impressing the life of each body she touches
she's a movie star, an icon, a history, a country,
expensive, compelling, free, sneaky, and yelling,
gorgeous and lovely, keep secrets and tell me,
she is my home, my mysterious dwelling
and in her I drown and emerge and keep sailing
      I wish I didn't want her

The Tiniest Difference

the cars are black
the phones are black
the suitcases are black
the pants are black
the dresses are black
the lingerie is black
the religious clothing is black
the formal clothing is black
it's hard to tell them apart
all the people, wearing all that black
with those black things, in those black things
the people all so similar
their needs identical
their wants all so particular and different
some of them want to punish
some of them want to love
they all need to eat
they all need somewhere to live
the borders are in their minds
their teams, their countries, their religions
the baggage comes down
spit out onto the carousel
traffic in the streets,
goods on the racks, on the shelves
all the people look for theirs
the tiniest difference
a scratch, a stain, a feature, an imperfection
separating it from all the rest

Exhibition

All the black clothes are in New York City,
a uniform to don or oppose. Look at the nudes
pose confidently before the eye, the lens.

The city is a costume, wear it out.
It is a stage, it is a play, learn its lines,
wait on them, cramming.

A person is a library of memories,
buildings made of stories, fleshed-out
countenance, a billboard of a life.

What are you advertising
with your weary face and witch's laugh,
your arsenal of negativity?

Pull the trigger, PTSD.
Everyone's sins are validated by the crimes
that were committed against them.

The city that never sleeps, catnaps together.
The subway's rhythm a lullaby anthem,
kinesthetic drug pulling us under:

To surrender is victory.
See the grass in summer, strewn with half-naked bodies
mopping up the sun, headphones in, shoes off, dozing.

Manna-hatta, the Lenape's hilly island leveled
by beast and man, before electricity, by hand
we put the skyline together again, electric city,

brick by brick, glass pane by pain, rising to the sky
so the original topography is recovered,
reflecting the bedrock like an encore.

You stand on the riverbank, part of the horizon,
challenging your part, torn down to be built up,
to the applause of traffic, construction, destruction,

the arc of the show-me-everything,
it says with its curtains
of light.

The Best Pick-Up Line I Ever Heard

I was young and beautiful
jerked around by subway's massive rhythm
most handsome boy watching me from across the car
bookish, glasses, lean, sharp features, strong jaw
humble clothes, simple but unique in presentation
his eyes ate me up, black pupils kissing me all over
he drew me in his mind, I was convinced I was there
finally, after much fidgeting, I returned his gaze
powerfully rejecting common subway etiquette
I stared back, let my eyes rest on him

We came to his stop
door opened with its melody
breaking our trance
before he slipped out, he came
to me seated opposite his exit, quickly
he leaned in, extended his hand giving
me a piece of candy
"You just look so sweet, have a piece of candy.
I work at Union Square Barnes & Noble."
He darted through the doors

I was swallowed, peristalsis
subway moves through the bowels of the city
enveloped by the tunnel of love
I accept its darkness
for a week I thought of him, unable to distract myself
from his tiny bit of sugar, his thrust toward me
before the doors shut him from his destination
how he managed to lure me
to the enormous bookstore
hungrily combing the floors, the isles

Determined to find him,
I must have emoted a plea;
another employee asked,
"Can I help you find what you're looking for?"
"Yes. Not a book but a person who works here."
"Oh." He replied exasperated,
"Did he give you a piece of candy?
Ah yes, he works in Fantasy, will be here at 2."
Madly impressed, I left -
now, only kind-of looking for him

Dreams

Eat with me
that apple, fig, cherry-
something that was a flower once

I have this bouquet for you,
a perfume to take like medicine,
breathe with me

I want to count your ribs
with my hands, smooth out the memories
of hurt in your muscles

Drink with me,
some juice steeped in Time,
let it change us together

I want to sleep with you
and remember our dreams, our times,
our bodies that bloom and wither

What is the difference
between dreams and memories?
We believe in our memories

I Like the Married

I like the married,
the married are poor

Poured out their souls
in search of a cure

For Desire's insatiable way,
an aisle hacked through the maze

Divorce is for rich people,
marriage, a curse

Curses are blessings
because some things are worse

Villa or Château

I woke before dawn in France,
next to my husband of sixteen years,
in an exquisite boudoir, deer hide bedspread
and rose-patterned walls, we were
visiting his cousins in the Midi-Pyrénées

I admitted in the dark, so far from home
I was growing bored of fucking him in New York,
so, was grateful to be fucked in a Château
on the French countryside, his exotic status fortification
for our bond, novelty pleases thrill seekers

I respond to his familiar touches
                        barely, though encouragingly
wanting him to work harder,
                        grateful for his continued interest
I return it, I can't resist him,
even when I'm petulant, or mad, or try to be mean,
I remind him to kiss me, too often we skip my favorite part

Still seduced by his scent, I take him in, we drift
until the rooster crows, seven o'clock
bells clang in the distance

I open the shutters to look upon fields draped in mist,
this landscape same as it was 1000 years ago
as was the bridge we crossed to get here

So much travels so far and I am so busy breathing
the sweet air damp with lavender, so foreign
compared to where we live: the river, fresh tar, exhaust,

breathing, wanting
to breathe more

My body working, blood, liver, lungs responding
to the neural drive to breathe, so much coordination
just to keep on living, time passes, things don't get easier
just different, I tell my husband that I don't think I can
have a job anymore, breathing takes so much effort

Later, over a bowl of coffee and bread, he explained
it was not a Château, it was a Villa
but he didn't want me to miss a night in a Château
so, he let me sleep in a Château
and for this I love him

A Poem I Wrote in the Future

I was in my 40s when the days started disappearing
life became long nights, days shorter and shorter

I would wake, in minutes the day would be over,
only my most strict habits would be accomplished

I made coffee I never got to drinking
wrote for my novel, unedited it grew without shape

spent time listening, watching, loving my three children
failed at getting them to bed before 10 PM

I did yoga, my house was clean, beds made
Christmas decorations stayed up over a month

I practiced my songs and kept up with correspondence
fell behind at work, missed weird charges on my credit card

The sun rose and set as if the planet had shrunk
days blurred, night stretched, and I hungrily occupied it

Only the dark body of night could hold me
I became daytime's orphan and looked for my mother

I saw her face in the mirror, heard her voice from my throat
I felt my grandmother's expression on my mouth

My body has been replaced so many times this lifetime
I have done so much but so much more is undone

Can a human unbecome, lose the sun?
When did the rays become poison? Sunblock in everything

All those that made me, surface through my skin,
my children look just like me when I was that age

The calendar makes no sense and hours are erratic,
the math doesn't work out, the problems static, unsolved

selves shed, ghosts surround, mourning morning,
it gets harder to differentiate between victory and defeat

I stand like my dad, my husband recedes into his computer,
our children raveled into adults, we lost the apartment,

the phone replaced everything, the America experiment
failed, no one smokes cigarettes or cares about high-fidelity

I am as lonely as I was as a child, as I was all along,
the dream, the night, goes on and on and on

The Price of Love is War

I love you so much,
you make me understand war
Love's what we're always fighting for

Love is the crime and the fight
Love is the darkness, Love is the light
it hurts to not see Eye to Eye

We want so much
to be
the same

Same home, same bed, same children
same laws, same rights, same wrongs
same food, same beliefs, same songs

Same eyes at night: to stare, to hold
same arms, same lengths
Don't look so close

Keep some distance
keep some for yourself
the Have-Nots want, the Haves have wealth

We can't go back
in time, we can just keep going,
going, gone

Foreshadow Boxing

Sometimes I feel it
when no one is there

the blow of a punch
the shock of impact

the slap, the thud
metallic taste of blood

tooth-ringing bite
to my own insides

breath taken away
the dumbing collide

I know it is coming
I will be knocked down

Aftermath

Obscure sequence: fat lip, bloody knee
One lost night totaling eternity

Years versus minutes, it doesn't add up
The constant is tainted as variables corrupt

Her solution is poison and falsifies results
Not good at tests and riddled with faults

Congruence interrupted by carryover excesses
Quotient of attempts, remainder of messes

Mistakes carried forward, errors divert
A wreckage of prizes lost in the hurt

Coefficient of failure, absolute of defeat
Heart of subtractions, body of meat

A fraction replaced her, betraying their arc
There will be no credit for showing the work

The Letter B

Children study the parts of flowers
at school, they pull apart the real thing,
pin it down to show their knowledge.

We are taught to destroy the things
we want to prove we know.

On the exam, they must label
the names on drawings.
Their yellow pencils tap and bob.

Only poets can diagram
what the flower truly is.

Photographs lie and scientists
leave out everything important.
You can hear the bees in the poem,

and my full haunches are forfeited
in your travels to catalog species.

You miss feeding me your blueberries,
no matter how many other tongues
you put them on, none taste like mine.

L

L, I put you in all my children's names
because you sit so patiently and tall, talk calm,
sometimes you're silent, sometimes soft consonant
your comforting sound, a lingering languishing lull when
time moves too fast your right angle provides stability,
your sound makes the tongue kiss the teeth
L, you're in Love and Lust and Luck,
in cursive you loop, loaded, lush, legendary,
you lavish, longitude, latitude, leather, and lace
your light licks lollipops of licorice laughs,
lounging lilting little things like days in lives so small
amassing, getting fat with time, long, late
you are three o'clock, you are midnight, you are noon
lean olden L, everyone gets to be young
but being old is the grand prize after all,
any promotion means more work
winning is a trick, a bigger job, a Tom Sawyer prank,
that's why capital L sits, it's tired
from standing up in all those lowercase situations,
boomerang-like, L always coming back for more
it keeps its back straight at attention
fits in a corner comfortably
doesn't back down.

Balloons

"How many balloons are floating around
lost in outer space?" asks my son,
four orbits around the sun, he has let go at least a dozen,
latex or Mylar pulling tears from his eyes
as gravity is defied. Rise, rise, a helium trait.
Do we heal after loss or just change?

Balloons break hearts:

99 Luftballons 1984, *The Red Balloon* 1956,
Ours, lost over the Cote d'Azur, an open window
impelled such punishment.
Post the apocalyptic aftermath of loss every day,
something must rise, we are drawn to those
and we want more from them than what they can.

He keeps going back for more, pleading for them,
no matter how many times the balloons disappoint him.
If they don't escape and shrink into the distance,
or tangle in a tree, they slowly sink and shrivel,
or worse, POP, startle, terrify.

The planets around their stars, so much helium themselves-
Who says there are no balloons in outer space?
Explanations fail us,
imagination is not something to be proved.
I just tell him, "All the lost balloons are there,
all of them."

Arlene

I had two cousins named Arlene,
I only realized it when I was 50
and they were sitting on the couch
together for the first time.

One was from my mother's
side of the family, my favorite cousin,
the other was from the side of dreams.
It was Arlene, as a little girl,

so that we'd always get to play
kick-the-can on Long Island
with all the kids on Naples Lane
and enjoy the game Monopoly

and watch The Wizard of Oz on TV.
No matter how I see that movie,
it's me watching with her, as children
on our bellies in my grandma's rec room,

our chins propped up on our hands,
the Berber carpet, wood paneling on the walls.
That room is long gone but I still occupy it:
the bar with three stools

and the white round table from Italy
with four black and red chairs
where we wrote Christmas cards
and licked every stamp.

I can still taste the glue,
and hear the phone ring,
a real mechanical bell shaking inside
to make the sound.

The vibration of a thing echoes
so that I have so many
cousins Arlene,
one from every time we spent together,

like the time we tried to rub out the blood
from the bedding when I got my period
but the evidence couldn't be erased.

Sheet

flower petal of my bed,
sheet, you cover me
absorbing my dreams,
my sweat, my oil, my tears
I leave myself soaked into you
you get so soft, stained, old
you become the sail for the ship
of my son's skateboard
you become the ghost
costume on Halloween
you lie on the beach for me
to lounge in the sun, feeling
the warm sand beneath you,
imprint of my body there and how
I wrapped my babies in you
hammock-like, to swing them around,
hear them squeal with laughter
I remember when I was small,
my mother did the same thing to me,
the sheet flapped like a great flag
on the clothesline in the breeze,
we would drape it over chairs
to become a fort to hide in,
or a curtain for a play,
a sheet can be so much more
than what it was intended to be,
it is our greatest strength, to expand
things beyond their initial purpose

Tell Lies

Tell lies,
lie, lie, lie.
They say, lies destroy the world
but lies make the world.
There are so many lies
they are actually holding the truth together.
Without lies, no one would understand the truth.
Just lie, to protect the people you love
from pain.
Just lie, to protect yourself,
it's so easy to disappoint people.
Just tell them what they want to hear, lies!
Tell yourself lies
to hold your narrative together,
otherwise, you'll lose hope and hate yourself.
Your promises are lies
because no one knows the future.
Promises address the mess of your conflicting aspirations,
to comfort yourself and those you care for.
Your explanations are lies
constructed to justify your insatiable hunger,
your insurmountable desire, dealt at birth
for no reason, no meaning, but for what you make up.
Fact is, religion is a lie, history is a lie, reality is a lie,
they are agreements on elaborate fictions
that create a map for an infinity that cannot be mapped;
except for the map itself is the existence!
No one wants the truth.
If they say they want the truth, they are lying.
Go ahead, tell them the truth
and they will call you a liar.

Self-Study

I'm an endangered species
there is only one of me
I already died
except for the ones in captivity

and that me in a cage
that's not really me
that's whoever
has the key

I have been so many
to so many
things I wanted
and things they'd tell me

I'll say yes to you
mother mystery
grateful for my arms
and armies

my sides my allies
that you have touched
held my clothes up
and undressed me

a study to be free
every last drop of the body
the bodies we get to be
the ones we become

never to keep

Lion's Den

You only think you own something,
there are only doorways to rented rooms,
our bodies are borrowed,
waking up is impossible, yet
we do it every day

Orphans and lovers have nowhere,
so, belong everywhere, like lions,
not long in any den but the veld belongs to them
since the late Pleistocene epoch
they roam free

The homeless have the ceiling of the stars
at night in Grand Central Station,
corridors their destinations
instead of passageways, and they
are stock-still while bankers rush ours

Who gets to thrive? Who gets to struggle?
Who waits in prison for a trial for years
and is proven innocent? Who is guilty?
You never get back time, and it's all we have.
There is nowhere for us beasts to go.

A Line

A line
is for reading
is for waiting on
is for dividing a page
is for coke

A line
is for drawing
is for hooking the fish
is for coloring in
is for drying clothes

A line
is to memorize
is to walk on
is to drop
is to send voltage across

A line
is a dress cut
is my subway home
is the punch of the joke
front line, lifeline, fault line

A line
is to follow
line-dance, line haul
Get out of line
a line is to cross

Sexier Than God

Dear God, the Devil is sexier than you-
the Devil looks so hot in pictures and movies,
I want to make out with king of the bad boys.
My flame! Smile lascivious, I want
to know the fiery kiss from his burning lips.
He's all red and black, pointy horns, huge cock.
Ravenous, he's ripped, muscular tight,
every cell trembling with the agitation of life.

Dear God, the Devil is hungrier than you-
I want to eat with someone hungry, for that is when food
tastes best, I want to devour the apple, play with the snake
and climb in the tree, I want to count bones with my eyes,
then my fingers, then tongue. Everything is doomed,
Dear God, the Devil is lonelier than you-

in the name of God, you get the credit
even when men paint with the Devil's own palette,
the Devil's signature acts justified by you! He's just
a supporting role in your world domination blockbuster,
Monotheism, that hijacked human culture,
misogyny grandfathered in, tax-exempt status,
the eternal recurrence of the same events
thus spoke Zarathustra, Oh Aten, dear God

You are all politics and prescription, holy books and
religion, requisition of Love and Righteousness mere
shields and bait to justify hate and make us wait
for your myth of heaven, that only belittles that which
Earth has given, dear God, the Devil is sexier than you-
and through his sexiness, I'm sexier too.

Sexy Roman

> *"Only to the extent that we expose ourselves*
> *over and over to annihilation can that which is*
> *indestructible in us be found."*
>   *-Pema Chodron*

So sexy, she lost her head
and her arms and legs.
Those lines of her torso though,
her thighs scissoring apart
are enough.

That edge of tunic pulled taut
from her kinetic pose, so delicate-
such an accomplishment
for the heavy density
of marble to convey.

Curves of her shoulders alone
tell us the weight of her arms,
sinistro reaching back,
destro arcs forward.
Her supple stone breast

bursts with her heart
for thousands of years now.
Could you hear it beating
if you cupped your warm ear
to the cool mineral bust?

Unleash light
from solid blocks of Earth
honed by carving
tools. Our arms
shape arms from the elements

with the elements. We chip away
at the source, the damage
reveals the dream.
Mortals have
such powerful imaginations.

We need so little but want
so much. We tear ourselves apart
with desire and we manifest
through the violence of a kiss.
This is what I mean

when I ask you to destroy me.
Look at how the beautiful bodies last
through time, mere remnants
conjuring the whole,
our sorrow and our triumph.

The Wanting

the wanting gets me tired
the wanting wakes me
the wanting makes it hard to fall asleep
the wanting shapes my dreams
the wanting keeps me here
wanting to see it always
never able to see it enough or have it enough
wanting to memorize every second
knowing the mind is too small to do so
knowing this scant space of time here is all we have
to love with and we want it we want it we want it
the wanting is the water
that nourishes, bathes, and drowns
rains, floods, and evaporates
trickles, sings, and crashes
and gushes and courses through
our delicate little veins

Fine Night

We could walk side by side
twin rhythm down stairs
match steps, stare
light matches, hold hands
ignite, share lands, press lips, hips
I could flood your body, eyes, and mind
soak up your time
we could commit the same crime
and I would still not be close enough

I could drink your blood
memorize your love
follow you, I could go into your skin
drench myself in
you and still
I would not be close enough
to have enough
of you, your golden brilliance
blurs my edges halo bright
floating astral body rocket fire flight

This universe so big
it will never be filled
it is not
finite

Wrong

Eventually, you find out you were wrong
about everything. Nothing stays right.
You're finally sure, and then
it switches all around:

The world is flat, then round
Women shouldn't work / Lady, get a job!
Square Meals changed to the Food Pyramid
        but now, Eat the Rainbow
Doctors recommend Camel Cigarettes
Chocolate, your vice, is good for you

You're much too beautiful to be wearing those shoes
A kiss turns out to be the middle finger

The hero becomes the villain
Your poem becomes your novel
Your novel becomes a postcard
Your mother becomes your child

Wait long enough, you'll find the favorite scarf
you thought you lost forever.
We become and keep becoming
because we're wrong.

Embers Kindle

I still feel the weight of you
as we lay Love's bloody mess bare
on the wood floor of a secret room

You fell asleep, panting, dreaming
in my arms on my body there
the full gravity of you understood

We are part of this city's landscape in time
like the last swamp cedar on West Street,
at once a memory and a dream, also, really there

Growing beside an ordinary building
harkening back to earlier days,
about to be snuffed out by modernity

Crush the tiny spine-leaf, sniff it from our fingers
soon to be thrust inside one another,
root into what is, to become what will be

Now, wood smoke in our hair from the bar,
the cast iron potbelly part of the original building,
special case but not to code, hazard, we survive

Still, my arms around you, whose face is in my eyes
I have you when you are not here
You belong to me when you are not mine

Theremin

You are my theremin
I have to play you without touching
your voice almost human-sounding
sensing
then singing

Electronic
we never get to touch
except in the music
we art together
in the avant-garde

Hardly anyone is listening
no one is dancing
it looks like magic
to play without touching
you, my theremin

Hands in the air
I have to admit
sometimes I just want to hold you
like an old-fashioned
instrument

The Way They Wanted

The way they wanted their mouths to fit,
image to line up, thoughts to map,
eyes to lock, and skin to snap

The way they wanted to please the other,
show the ropes, suspend the mother,
invert her body, world upside down

The way they ran away but stayed in town,
an antique factory, a bathroom stall,
a pier on her birthday, appear not to fall

They wanted so much, there was never enough,
playing soft, playing tough,
another whiskey, another smoke

The closer to truth, the bigger the joke
The way they wanted more than this life
The way they got it, despite the grief

How We Prey

Two wolves at night, airborne, hunting.
A Great Grey Owl watches.
Deer tracks pierced in snow.

I think it's the sex
that makes me love you so much,
but it's afterward when we talk

we discover we are captive
to the same favorite diorama
at the Museum of Natural History.

Luminescent, surprising in the dark just
after a turn down a narrow hall, panting
as the hunting pair, caught in the crosshairs.

Even

Even if you talk to me like I'm an idiot
and you're short-tempered because
my grand statements abrade you today
Even if you give me a hard time
because you heard this story already
Even if you are annoyed by my talk
of current events because you read
the paper cover to cover yourself anyway
Even if you belittle my interpretation
and we just don't agree but you claim
it's because I don't understand
and you accuse I simplify everything
Even if you're in a bad mood
because you're hungry, I'm hungry too
and we both drank too much on empty
Even if we are impossible and wrong,
hedonist, atheist, selfish, and magical
Even if you make me cry because I'm sensitive
and female and full of whiskey and wild
Even if we compete because it's our nature
Even if you're falling apart and have no insurance
Even if we're in pain and you doubt me
Even if you cane my feet and make me wince
Even if you get black tufts of hair growing on your body
that shoot out of the holes in your shirt
I still love you even if we can't control ourselves
Even if we can't control, even if we can't control Love
I still, still Love you, you, Love, you don't choose Love
can't control Love still, still you, even if, even though

This Proves My Love

That which I weep, I'll never be free of.
Jaw dropped slack as death, on couch, asleep,
you've seen my ugly face; this proves my love.

Crush my soul with a spell, a curse, a shove
when doubt's cast from your eyes and words you speak,
that which I weep. I'll never be free of

You, your hemp, you bind my heart, tie me up
knots even undone. I eat what you make,
you've seen my ugly face; this proves my love.

Your ropes imprison me; I am your glove.
I'd visit you in prison every week,
that which I weep, I'll never be free of.

I let you suspend me, inform each move,
I write poems and porn for you, hide and seek.
You've seen my ugly face; this proves my love:

you've seen me cry, be mean, try, fail thereof.
I risk my life to let you use me; keep.
That which I weep, I'll never be free of.
You've seen my ugly face; this proves my love.

Automaton

I thought I was really alive
waiting for you the whole time
wondering if you'd ever be real

the Velveteen Rabbit,
Galatea and Pinocchio
warned me

the nursery Skin Horse explains
how it happens, Geppetto's workheart
Venus grants Pygmalion's wish

the beloved arrives from the yearning
clock hands can't hold onto anything
but they deliver us

this patient game
that reveals: it is fascinating to hold something
that cannot be held onto

and the more you try to dissuade me that I'm yours
the more I feel your arms around me and
we're breathing

Your Destination

You couldn't come home with me.
The signs confuse me, I have trouble
processing multiple names for roads and exits.
The fog covered the river that night, it was hard to see,
I blamed the weather, the GPS, I blamed
the myth of technology, my mood, the headlights,
and that I can't remember a list of directions.
I feel ashamed, angry at my limitations.
I fall short, I think everything fails, and I wanted it all
so bad. You, the way, the way I wanted,
the way I wanted you. You couldn't come home with me
because because because... a million reasons,
and there are always a million things to blame but
we do get all these days and sometimes things work out
really well, and sometimes even if they don't work out,
there is still beauty.

I got to the other side
without you when I wanted you with me,
but there was that part we were together in the car
for awhile, your face and your body with mine, and that
was so good and so great that I'll keep trying, I'll keep
waking up and going for it no matter how sorry I feel for
myself, or how much I cry with wanting. There's plenty
of good days even though we think there's not enough-
Don't think that, use your imagination more positively,
believe in the good parts, that they keep coming,
that they're on their way, we're getting closer.
I made it, despite all my mistakes and the emptiness that
fills me. I made it across the bridge and returned the car
without you. You couldn't come home with me and
we'll be together soon.

Though Obviously

though obviously
smarter, it's true,
I will not stop riding
the motorcycle,
I will continue
taking dangerous hikes solo
through rough terrain
shoulds and *musts* — unheeded
talks and warns — in vain

pick until infected
scratch until it bleeds
eat sugar, fat, salted butter
lose umbrella, find trouble
no helmet for the bicycle,
no life jacket for the canoe,
say too much, won't shut up,
hit   SEND   too soon

stay up late, sleep late,
smoke all kinds of things,
drink until silly, fall to pieces,
think my arms are wings,
fall to pieces, make myself
new

no matter how
much sense it makes,
I will not give up
you

You Are the Dream

You are the dream
that swims and feels cold
that gets sand in the car
and the bed and lays on the
sheets until they are rags
you spread on the beach
between you and the sand
where you dream after a swim
and warm up in the sun
until you are gone
you can keep swimming
impossible things keep
happening some days
are for swimming and sand
remember this cool skin
wet, evaporating
you are the dream
with the car and the sheets
with arms that paddle
legs that kick and go
swimming more
days like this, please
keep happening

La Petite Mort

I carry a little death with me
on my back, in my bag:
cigarettes, my poems,
my attempts at impossible hopes,
a lighter, illegal herb in a one-hitter,
dirty secret photos, poems by others,
folded love letters soaked by rain.

What is man but his problems?
A lifetimeline of mistakes,
knots on a rope a finite length,
we end at a loose end, forever
undone but finished,
we're left hanging by our dreams.

We never get enough of that sexy lover,
or the badass bass line, or the laughter
from our baby girl in the surf for the first time.
If only the sweet sound could sing forever
and I could keep the whiskey high,
the buzz on my lips from the kisses I need
as a mother, a wife, a lover, a human hungry
for things to stay the same- when everything's good,
but we're brought down again and again.

We continue our relationship
with gravity until the grave,
we're saved when we think we're saved.

Bouquet

The world that disappears,
that is the world we know

We are given beauty that becomes
the memory of beauty

We are given love and
the love letters are filed away

Oh, write me a letter,
remember when you wanted to,

when letters burned inside you
as you dreamed of me

You would pen them
or tap them out on a keyboard

how you planted letters in rows
to flood me, break me open, bloom

You were learning me by heart, Sunshine,
the babies blossomed

and became children.
One day, our teenage son said,

"Do you realize there was one day you picked me up, and
put me back down, and then never picked me up again."

The beauty endures
through seasons, selves

There is a thread of sameness
that sews the past to the present.

There is a world we do not know that is
coming to us, appearing with its flowers.

What we cease to carry,
carries us through.

Write it down.

I've been in the woods at night

with a bottle of Jack and a beautiful girl,

I know what it's like to be on top of the world,

been there a few times, that's why I stay,

I know it will be mine again someday

About the Author

Jane LeCroy grew up in Nyack, NY, and is a NYC-based poet, singer, performance artist, teacher, and home-birthing mother of three. Jane's work is in the permanent collections of the Smithsonian, Library of Congress, Poets House, Brooklyn Museum of Art, and Yale Library. Jane has been publishing student work and teaching writing, literature, and performance through various organizations, serving elementary school students through the university level. Jane fronts the avant-pop band, The Icebergs, and the spontaneous experimental music project, $\Omega\nabla$(Ohmslice) with Bradford Reed. She toured with the SF-based, all-women's poetry troupe, Sister Spit in the 1990s. Jane is a featured performer at Poetry Brothel. Among her many publications and recordings, her chapbook, "Names", was published by the art-book house, Booklyn, in the award-winning, ABC chapbook series, which was purchased by the Library of Congress along with her braid. Three Rooms Press published "Signature Play," a multimedia book of lyrical poems, including a nomination for a Pushcart Prize. The Icebergs and $\Omega\nabla$(Ohmslice) are both on www.ImaginatorRecords.com, available everywhere you stream music. Some of these poems appear as songs on her records from The Icebergs: "Eldorado" and "Add Vice."